sometimes lost, sometimes found

Adina Vlasov

sometimes lost, sometimes found © 2022
Adina Vlasov

All rights reserved.

No part of this publication may be reproduced, stored in a retrieval system, or transmitted, in any form or by any means, electronic, mechanical, photocopying, recording or otherwise, without the prior written permission of the presenters.

Adina Vlasov asserts the moral right to be identified as author of this work.

Presentation by *BookLeaf Publishing*

Web: www.bookleafpub.com

E-mail: info@bookleafpub.com

ISBN: 9789395969178

First edition 2022

DEDICATION

To Jack. You make me better every day.

january

it's that time of year
where dragging my tired bones out of bed
is both the hardest and first thing i must do

rebirth takes energy:
the shedding of old cells; unlearning
i trust the work is happening inwards

because out here is barren
2 black eyes greet me in the mirror
a clinical exhaustion

it's difficult to answer
     "what day is it?"
           "how are you?"
my fingers and feelings are frostbitten

but i'm here.
ready to burst through the chrysalis
as soon as spring allows

role reversal

role reversal:
you aloof and i awaiting
all done up, all dressed down -
does duty call?

flip the script:
sexily solipsistic
what do you mean you won't come,
here?

riding the train backwards
too tired for this shit
do what you will
i don't bend at your will

home life

the subtle, seductive drawl of domesticity
so frustratingly easy to fall into
blanket me up with a siren song
caught up in the arms
       of you, new beloved

lay with me / live with me
days blend together in idyllic idleness
so much coaxing in this warm embrace
why not turn in towards bliss?

bless the (shrinking) part of me
opening her eyes to see through this rosy veneer
turning out, up in arms
there is more to seek than this

journal entry no. 2

as i walk to get my morning coffee i am painfully aware of the space i take up. perhaps it's because fall settles on me with a weight; cardigans and cares. i take it with cream now because i'm allowed to be soft. i practice caressing instead of clawing.

let a body be a body. i glimpse my reflection and wish i hadn't. how to be loving - no, neutral, - which are we trying to be these days? "nothing tastes as good…" i feel most beautiful when the jeans fit loose. i tell myself it's a comfort thing.

//

i take the long way home and am painfully aware of the vacancy at my side. i fill every minute of my days so as to not feel the chasm; a safety net of beautiful people. mostly i enjoy sleeping alone; there is a piece of me that likes this peace in me. i am nobody's girl.

TTC

another belt loop down

i go from place to place
as if in a dream
remembering only moments in transit,
inbetweens

scanning platform faces
on the verge of familiarity
crowds bring this comfort
one foot then the other
white noise scores the scene

it seems i am always doing
but never getting anything done
frustrating frenzy
eaten from the inside out

another belt loop down

coffee as the sun comes up,
as the sun goes down
one foot then the other
when was the last time i took
a full breath?

i'd like to love everyone on this subway
i'd like everyone [on this subway] to love me
suddenly i'm nauseated
by the dizzying sway

sunsets

i witnessed my most beautiful sunsets at the edge of
seventeen.
rushing out on the front lawn of my childhood home
taking photographs of this precipice

brilliant strokes of pinks and oranges like i've never
seen since
there are still symphonies in the sky
but none grip me by the heart and pull
quite like the credits of my waning youth

as if mother nature had prepared a eulogy
for my passing into this next phase

~

i sit here years later.
i've yet to look up to find those impressionist
paintings smiling down on me

perhaps the venue is all wrong, or the stage

perhaps it's the director, with her glory days gone,
bowing gracefully out

perhaps it's the audience -
when did i stop applauding?

ill

trying to swallow my pride
but it hurts on the way down
and the way up; a new ladder.
i go out again and again,
lay down again and again

sweetness suddenly spiralling
into chaos i thought was controlled
forced to yield; my body is no fool
putting a pause on living
to stop me from dying

youth is not here to be abused -
yet predictably, cyclically
i bleed her dry
the id enamoured with invincibility

present living has its pitfalls.

tourist

handle with care:
for me, the box
for you, the contents

you fresh-faced tourist
still making your footprints on this earth
and yet a map is obsolete

intuition is a marvellous thing
so is chemistry
in this alchemy your hands are still haunting me

i'll guide you in darkness
in light -
no matter

you tilt my face up to yours and i dissolve

ritual

every morning i awake and make my bed
this is an act of kindness towards myself

gaping

i've looked away from my chest
but the gnawing
tear tracks
tired kisses
it's not about what might have been

hours tumble away
until suddenly i'm cradled
childhood home
back to basics
circling
we have less control over these things than we might
think

waves and waves
letting them blanket me
you come to me broken but healing
i come to you no longer numb
outpour
what a gift, to be sincere

thawed
i've looked away from my chest
but i feel it now
growing pains
you awful angel
i miss you i miss you i miss you

tactile

love is tactile
tracing circles along edges
of cups, faces
fingertips finding you
in new places:
perhaps tonight we'll sip the sunset
from a new roof

love is tactile
tracing lines up and down
two spines
words and wonder
both are mine
when is it too early to make the call?
three,
      two,
          one

journal entry no. 3

13

i can't remember not knowing you. i don't recall that
gradual slope of comfort that comes with time. there
is only a deep fondness stretching out as far as the
eye can see.

//

to wait until curtain call
as we bow and exit this stage
of life
to tell you (or tell you not)

i had years
with you cast alongside me
letting me shine
the spotlight finding you anyway
we are a product of production

i mourn not the end of the run
but the way we float apart without it
to break my own heart -
not calling love by its name
until it's far too late

to pluck the last petal
(he loves me) he loves me not

midnight musings

jolted into a change of scenery
welcome, as all beginnings are,
but not known as such.
neurotic newness

long past bedtime
familiar faults (dulled)
acutely controlled
keeping me gazing at the skyline

why am i thinking of you
even in this state?
cursing my condition
the ease of falling in love

is it even about me?
do i just love to love?
extending tenderness to a warm body
but yet you are everything i need

everything i've been missing
i don't think it's fair
assigning you this role
the ideal is that we Be.

I should like to Be.
i should like to truly Be.
how do you feel?
i'd like to be more in tune

mother's day

at first, a love unchosen
the suckle of necessity
keeping me to your heart
the endless waking hours -
"day" and "night" -
these words hold no meaning to me
a baby so eager to be in the world
that i left you before my time

in time, the gradual divide
good/bad
fun/strict
i am so sorry now
but at six knew no better
i put you in a box
as he put you in a box
when you should have been free
(i'm so glad you are free)

fast forward, teenage tantrums
madly mercurial
there is no textbook for this
me, searching for approval (everywhere but in
your arms)
you, fighting your own battles

meanwhile the little wolf needing
in a more tangible way than i was needing
i do not blame
but i do hurt

now, a gentle mending
of both our hearts
it is so hard to be a woman
but oh, how we reap the rewards
when there is a harvest
i wouldn't trade it for the world
i choose to love
from a place of wholeness
from your own i see you reaching
out to me and unto me

we are one flesh,
my mother and i

red velvet

cake for breakfast, you for lunch
sweetness on your terms
we learn each other quickly, effortlessly

a sweetness that i've yearned:
years of rice crackers and sitting three feet apart
on the couch
as if decadence a sin

the proverbial sweet tooth shamed away - but why?
there is nothing holier than thou,
holding me in tow

the problem with pleasure:
how can you know you are worthy of it?

i lick my fingers clean.

lifeline

to be without doing
to do without pleasing
to please without feeling
to feel without healing
(a cycle impeding)
i'm safe when you're near me
but he's in the cracks
of my vulnerable acts
ignoring the wreckage
expecting the carnage
a lifetime of haunting
a lifeline your offering -

to be without fearing
to need without reason
to hold and be held without begging and
bleeding
the haven you foster
the heaven i'm after
to do as i'm pleasing
to know that i'm healing

haiku

choosing to open
a passive process, really
letting the light in

never have i ever

a smile inked on my face
holding close like i held you
this image in my mind.
the sun kissing my skin / you kissing my nose
dear spring, you are so welcome here

i think of all the butterflies
invisible strings
getting our lips to touch
i don't think i'd mind much
if we were just God's puppets

to live in a dream,
swimming in your eyes
with time no longer ticking
how could we have forecasted
a gravity like this?

may

the month of may throws me a wink and a smile.
i am stepping into a new confidence with you
walking beside me holding my hand; the
unspoken truth that neither of us will let go.

the warm breeze runs its hand through my hair
like a lover.

summer is for sleeping with the window open.
for the sweet smell of sunscreen and campfire
smoke lingering on sweaters as you linger on my
mind.

"i love you"

the phrase tastes sweet in my mouth - as i find
yours over and over. i could stare into the bright
blue pools of your eyes until the earth stops
moving.

gilded

twin fire signs. no wonder we thrive this time of year. i watch with eager eyes as the Sun stretches His stiff legs and runs further and further towards the Night. She loves this game, inching the finish line further and further with each passing day.

i too love this game. feeling the warmth as the evening slips unnoticed. until we find ourselves sitting in a park bathed in gold thinking it's still the afternoon.

late light sneaks in through my window to introduce itself and gives me the sweetest surprise. the waiting is not so hard when i know each day it will kiss my cheeks if i stand in just the right corner of my room. i will stand and wait and stand and wait until those kisses can once again come from you.

11:11

the wish is the same:
"you, forever"
a mantra

love is redundancy
repeating myself
like clockwork

sacred rituals
smiling at stories i've heard before
this practice becomes me

the infinite currency
of kisses, caresses
of saying "i love you"

the wish is the same:

"you, forever"

                    "you, forever"

          "you, forever"

www.ingramcontent.com/pod-product-compliance
Lightning Source LLC
LaVergne TN
LVHW010024200726
843495LV00015B/1913